PRACTICAL BUSINESS –
ABC

What people are saying about Practical Business - ABC

This book combines business theory and practice
to encourage readers to take action. The range of case
studies involving business personalities is particularly
insightful and provides inspiration to those who aspire
to running their own businesses.
Very easy to understand and quite enjoyable too.
*Mavis Amankwah, Award Winning Entrepreneur, Author
& PR Guru, Managing Director of Rich Visions*

I had a first read of Practical Business - ABC,
and my favourite, most impacting and poignant
chapter was the one on 'Networking'.
Why Networking, you might ask, or better still, what's the
big deal about Networking?
However the question is asked, Andrea brings to life the
very essence and practicability of doing business.
*Oluneye Oluwole, Development and Media Consultant,
Author, Founder Adopt a Child Today Foundation*

Practical Business ABC is easy to follow, its
contents are very clear and well laid out; it is accessible
and empowering to the reader and written in a style that is
easy for an ordinary person to understand.
*Seymour Mattis, Executive Director (Teacher and HR
Professional), VITAL EET - Educational Training
Organisation.*

PRACTICAL BUSINESS – ABC
A Guide for Budding Entrepreneurs

Andrea M. Campbell, MBA MA

Publisher: AA Global Sourcing Ltd
Website: http://www.aaglobalsourcing.com

Second Edition

First published in Great Britain in 2010 by
The Book Guild Ltd

Pavilion View
19 New Road
Brighton, BN1 1UF

A catalogue record for this book is available from
The British Library

ISBN 978-1-4716-4289-0

*I would like to thank the following people
who contributed towards making this
publication possible:*

*My family – Richmond and Shari – for their
understanding and patience.*

*Jeremy Green of Business Link for his input
and expertise.*

*John Graham of Grahame Laurent Associates
for his expertise, advice and support.*

Contents

Introduction

Imagine having an exciting and rewarding career that provides you with an opportunity to consistently apply your creativity, drive and talents while making a living doing what you love. If you have the aspiration, desire and determination to own and manage a successful business, then this book is for you!

The ideas expounded in these chapters are based on key principles of entrepreneurship. They draw on the training and experience of the author (in particular in her role as Director of ACT Training Services), but more importantly on the experiences of over twenty well-known, successful businesspeople/entrepreneurs. The areas presented are by no means exhaustive and nothing should replace your gut feelings when it comes to business. The intention is to highlight some important factors to consider when you are planning to embark on a business venture or if you have recently started your own business.

Entrepreneurs and businesspeople come from all walks of life and have different backgrounds and life experiences. They are challenged to balance decision-making with risk-taking and they have to be ready for emerging opportunities. Effective preparation begins with oneself and chances are, if you are perusing this book, you are ready to take your first steps.

Starting and managing your own business is potentially one of the most fulfilling, challenging and rewarding careers of all. It takes a lot of hard work and long hours, but it is absolutely worth the effort.

Starting your own business? Factors to consider first

Starting your own business is one of the most important decisions you will make in your life. The key word as you embark on this journey is PREPARATION. Have a look at the following list as you prepare to take this very important step:

1   *Prepare your mind* – Think about why you want to start your own business. Do you have the discipline, the drive and commitment necessary? Do you have the right skills (both hard and soft); do you have the support? Do you believe you can succeed in business and are you committed to hard work? Do you have the backing of your family and have you considered how a change in your lifestyle will affect your family and your social life?

2   *Prepare your product or service* – What will you be selling? What are the features and more importantly, the benefits, of what you are offering? Have you identified a need for the product or service? How is your product different from those of your competitors? Why should customers come to you?

3   *Prepare for your market* – Is there a market for your product or service? What is its size? Who are your customers? Remember, customers are

not only those who buy the product; it is also those who use the product. Who are your competitors? What are your strengths, weaknesses, opportunities and threats (SWOT analysis) and how will they help or hinder your entry into the market? What are your strategies for overcoming existing and potential barriers? How will you price your product – will you be targeting the high end or the low end of the market? What will your website look like and when will it be ready? What are your routes to market? How will you advertise?

4   *Prepare your business model* – What is the name of the business? Has it been incorporated? What kind of organisation will it be, e.g. sole trader, limited liability company, a social enterprise, a franchise, etc. Do you understand the differences between these types of businesses? What will your organizational chart look like? Is it strictly hierarchical or does it have a flat structure?

5   *Prepare your resources* – Think about what you will need to get started. Do you have an appropriate place to work? Even if you are working from home, you will need to allocate space for your activities. Do you have access to enough financial resources to start up and cover your expenses (both personal and business) for at least three months? (You should not rely on loans at this early stage.) Do you have or have access

to personnel to help you, whether as volunteers, advisers or paid staff?

6 *Prepare your business plan* – This will help to orientate you and will facilitate access to loans if they become necessary. Write down your strategies and objectives. Include milestones, make assumptions and be truly realistic. Treat the plan as a working document, updating regularly and making changes as you learn, and in light of external environmental factors. You can start your business without the plan but try to formulate one as soon as possible.

7 *Prepare your financial projections* – Be aware of your financial position, especially your cash-flow. In the early stages you will need to avoid running into debt and incurring unnecessary costs in the form of interest and other penalties for late payments. Ensure you have in place a solid financial system which allows you to track every penny owed to you as well as the amounts owed to your creditors and ensure that you pay within agreed timescales.

8 *Prepare your systems* – It is almost impossible to run a successful business without the use of technology. Ensure that you have the relevant hardware and software to facilitate your processes. For example, you may need a computer with word-processing and spreadsheet software to communicate with stakeholders,

process your correspondence and help you keep track of your financial situation. As your business grows your systems should also improve to keep up with the volume of sales and/or customers that hopefully will be generated.

9   *Prepare your policies* – It is important to lay out 'ground rules' early. Depending on the nature of your business, these may include policies covering health and safety, equal opportunity, quality assurance, environment, finance, disability, staff (e.g. recruitment, induction, appraisal, disciplinary procedures) complaints and appeals, volunteering and child protection. It may also be useful at this stage to establish your core beliefs, mission, vision and values. If you don't have all your policies documented, do not let this stop you from starting your business. However, by the time you can afford to buy in help do try to have them in place.

10   *Prepare to work with people* – Even if you will not be employing staff right away, you will still need to work with people. For example, you may require the services of an accountant, sales and marketing personnel, and an administrator (especially if you are not very experienced with the computer). In addition, you may wish to discuss your plans with your bank and, depending on the product or service you are offering, you could need a lawyer. Decide who

you will need and establish a relationship with
them.

11   ***Prepare*** *to meet your statutory and other
obligations* – Develop an understanding of your
responsibilities as they relate to the filing of your
returns to Companies House. These include
National Insurance, Income Tax, Corporation
Tax, business rates and VAT regulations. Your
accountant will be able to assist you, but be
mindful that his (or her) costs are commensurate
with the amount of work he or she does for you.
You must also apprise yourself of employment
law, disability regulation, health and safety
regulation; types and levels of insurance, equal
opportunity and environmental laws. In addition,
your particular industry may have regulations
that apply to your sector. Ensure that you are
aware of these and put in place systems to
facilitate compliance. Be aware that ignorance
will not be an excuse from any consequences that
may arise from non-compliance.

12   ***Prepare*** *for your life to change* – In the same
way that the birth of a child changes your life,
your business is also your baby and will change
your life. Prepare for your priorities to alter, and
always keep in mind the need to have a work/life
balance. Especially in the early stages, when you
are all fired up with enthusiasm, you can lose
sight of what is truly important – the people in
your life.

5

If you are satisfied that you have sufficiently PREPARED to take the plunge, take it! Remember, an eaglet will never learn to fly until he is prepared to risk the jump.

1 Attitude

Our attitude is reflected in how we relate to people and situations. They are impacted by the beliefs, values and assumptions we hold.

In business, be careful how you relate to people. There will be no shortage of temptations to lash out or make a rash decision. One careless moment can cost a lifetime of regrets. One bad incident with a customer will be retold over and over with a potentially disastrous multiplier effect.

Businesspeople not only sell goods and services; they also build relationships. By building rapport and nurturing relationships you can get things done more easily. You are better able to satisfy your customers even if you are unable to grant their every wish. The difference between success and failure is often down to the qualitative characteristics of your product as a whole. These qualities must permeate the entire relationship – pre-sales, sales and post sales. They must be accompanied by a positive attitude which in turn will have a positive impact on your staff and be reflected in the way they treat customers.

When you make mistakes, try to remedy them. You may try compensating the individual. Ask yourself, how much would a free consultation, or a replacement item cost? Now compare that with how much you could lose if the customer shares their 'bad experience' with others. In most cases, if you let the customer 'win' you gain in the longer term.

A good attitude to your employees and colleagues is important. People are your greatest assets; do not take them for granted. Show your workers you care by giving praise when due, encouragement where necessary and positive feedback as often as possible. Try to be constructive when you give feedback, and avoid mixed messages and sanctions. Instead, offer guidance and support and empower people by giving them responsibilities and the resources to get the job done. Learning to listen and take advice also contributes to a positive attitude as it will help you recognise your own limitations and get people on board who can complement your skills and help you develop a successful business.

Many entrepreneurs leave school without business qualifications. Many more leave formal education without any recognised qualifications and find that they have a burning desire to do business. A positive attitude is particularly helpful in these circumstances. It attracts people, ideas and resources that you will need to bring your dream to life. An optimistic mindset fosters personal growth that is vital as you build your reserves and develop strength of character. Peter Jones, British business tycoon and founder of Phones International Group advises: 'Before writing a business plan, finding finance and launching forth, entrepreneurs must have the right attitude. As an entrepreneur, you must prepare yourself and your mindset'. Essentially, if you doubt your ability to succeed, you won't succeed.

Entrepreneurs often face stressful situations that are unprogrammed with no clear path to a solution. Staying positive allows you to develop a supportive environment that will help you focus, especially when negative thoughts enter your mind and you feel like giving up. It is commonplace for those who own and run businesses to fail on their first attempt. Indeed, there are many examples where entrepreneurs sustain losses with their first, second and even third business venture and still eventually go on to make it big, satisfying their thirst for success.

Colonel Harland Sanders, founder of Kentucky Fried Chicken, was rejected over 1,000 times as he made his sales calls. Yet he maintained a positive attitude and was resilient, and today the KFC brand is one of the most recognisable in the world.

When you adopt a positive attitude, you will be better able to cope with the challenges that emerge as you strive to improve your business. When you are clouded by negative attitudes you won't be able to see the opportunities lurking in the shadows.

Key points:
- ✓ *Maintain a positive attitude – to staff, customers, suppliers and others.*
- ✓ *Practise active listening and take advice where appropriate.*
- ✓ *Adopting a positive attitude enables you to cope better with challenges.*

2 Buyer

The 'buyer' in this context is referring to the customer. Your customers must be at the forefront of your thoughts. It is not about what you want to sell, or what you think they need. Rather, it is more about what they want to buy. Think less about their 'needs' and more about their 'wants'. For example, people need to eat fruit and vegetables but they still want junk food. In many cases they eat junk food far more often than vegetables, despite the potential adverse impact on their health. The price has little to do with the products they buy; indeed it may be cheaper to buy fruits and vegetables, but they still *want* fast food. Who are you to tell them otherwise?

In our training company – ACT – we offered a range of programmes that we thought were good for our target clients – unemployed people seeking to acquire skills to access employment opportunities. We packaged the programmes well and engaged highly trained and experienced trainers. It became clear early in the programme that some courses had no takers. Feedback from clients revealed that they were not interested in them as they did not deem them necessary and could not appreciate their value. Despite our feelings on the matter we had to change the programmes.

Customers want goods and services to meet their requirements. They expect value for money. They expect an efficient after-sales service. They expect to be treated with respect; with warm and friendly service, whatever form that service may take – telephone, face-to-face, online, or in writing. When people buy a product or service, they are buying benefits, value and satisfaction.

This feel-good factor does not end with the purchase. It continues into the after-sales service – prompt attention to complaints, refunds or exchanges and the fulfilment of pre-purchase promises. Customers want to feel important; they want to be listened to and taken seriously. If possible, refer to them by name – that gives them a feeling of being special.

Train your staff to be helpful. Customers do not like to hear the words 'no', 'I don't know', or 'it can't be done'. It's not always possible to say 'yes' to a customer or do exactly what they want; however, it is important to be as flexible as you can. Customers need solutions to their problems and a 'no' answer does not help to put things right.

When things do go wrong, fix them promptly and, if possible, compensate your customers. They will forgive your mistakes if you bounce back quickly and effectively. Customers will usually come back if you keep your promises, provide a service of a high standard and inspire confidence. Treat them as individuals and you will make it easy for them to do business with you. They want to hear a friendly voice at the end of the telephone, not continuous instructions of buttons to press, which simply add to their frustration.

Consumer expectations are rising in the increasingly competitive business arena. If you are unable to satisfy your customers, someone else will. In today's business environment, retaining your customer base is key to business success. If you don't give your customers good reasons to stay, your competitors will offer them good reasons to leave. Customer retention and satisfaction drive profits. It is much easier to work with your existing customers selling more goods and services to them than it is to attract new customers. Once you have the trust of customers you will find it easier to penetrate your existing markets.

Customers buy for different reasons, but in most cases they seek products and services that best suit their requirements. A product does not need to be rated highest in all respects by customers – only in those they think important. For example, many people are keen to have a mobile phone in order to make and receive calls and text messages. To many, the enhanced features of sending emails or downloading ringtones are less important. With the exception of those who love technology, the needs of most people are satisfied with a phone that sends and receives calls, text and voice messages, and stores telephone numbers.

David Gold, a self-made millionaire who, along with his brother Ralph, owns Gold Group International, one of the most profitable private businesses in the UK, explains that 'you have to supply your customer or you die' in his book *Pure Gold – Rags to Riches*. This highlights the sheer importance of recognising what the customer wants and supplying it. He is pointing out there can be a thin line between life and death when it comes to business.

Dale Carnegie, the famous American writer and lecturer, in his 1953 book, *How to Win Friends and Influence People* argues, 'the only way on earth to influence other people is to talk about what they want and show them how to get it'. It is as true now as it was then – half a century ago. How then can that concept be applied to business? How about engaging people in what

THEY want (not what we think they need), and supplying them with it?

By focusing on the needs of other people, Anthony Robbins, noted American professional speaker and author, changed his life from living in a run-down apartment in California, barely surviving on his pay cheque, to becoming a millionaire, several times over.

Brand loyalty is fast diminishing; indeed, it could be argued it is now a thing of the past. Customers want high quality and exceptional service. This results in greater customer retention, which in turn results in higher profitability. Customer loyalty contributes significantly to sustainable profit growth. As businesses grow, they can lose focus on the customer and start focusing on the profits. They seek ways to cut costs, often at the expense of the customer. They forget that key to business is creating value for customers and promoting customer satisfaction. Satisfied customers will be loyal customers who patronise your business, regardless of the competition. Although there are factors that influence customer loyalty, that loyalty will be secured by continuous customer satisfaction, which leads to repeat business.

Forward-thinking organisations seek to partner with their customers. By partnering with them, organisations take into account customers' views when developing new products or services. By partnering with your customers, you will be able to anticipate their needs way ahead of the competition. Say, for example, you are running a training organisation for further education. It

would be good practice to involve your clients in future
course development and progammes by asking them

what they would like to see on offer and listening to them. Shaping the course in line with their requests and sourcing the appropriate accreditations would meet with approval.

Competition forces companies to become more creative and flexible in their dealings with customers. Partnering with customers will help your organisation to remain focused in order to make good decisions and harness the commitment you need to survive when times are hard.

Key points:
- ✓ **Give buyers what they want.**
- ✓ **Train your staff to be helpful.**
- ✓ **Go beyond your customers' expectations.**
- ✓ **Involve your customers in product development.**

3 Creativity

Today's entrepreneurs are in constant search of effective means to attract customers and deliver their goods and services to them. Customer loyalty is no longer guaranteed, especially when customers have such a wide range from which to choose.

How can you ensure you get your slice of the pie? You can do this by being different, trying new approaches and challenging norms. If there are a few problems you cannot solve, or goals you cannot achieve, try applying your creative ability. Make sure you involve your staff in generating ideas because creativity knows no boundaries.

Creativity seeks to break out of the mindset that states that things cannot be done differently. It challenges fixed ideas such as, 'this is how it has always been done; it is working so why change it?' Start looking for multiple solutions rather than settling for the first, and perhaps most obvious one, and give yourself permission to be playful and inquisitive, flexible and versatile. When asked to outline a few rules for success, British-Asian businessman and multi-millionaire, James Caan said: 'Observe the masses and do the opposite'. Entrepreneurs often swim against the tide.

Creative thinking is a relatively novel concept and plenty has been written on the subject in recent years. However, certain ideas are fundamental to thinking creatively:

1. Don't let assumptions stifle your creativity. Challenge assumptions and norms – ask yourself, 'what if I were to try this?'
2. Actively seek alternatives. Stay open and generate as many options as you can think of before deciding on one.
3. To generate solutions, create an atmosphere where you and others feel comfortable expressing new ideas. Discourage a forum where weaker ideas are unfavourably evaluated or attacked.
4. Look for wider solutions; shed inhibitions and move from left brain (logical thinking) to right brain (creative thinking).
5. Think sideways and explore the least likely directions. Abandon step-by-step approaches and replace them with creative ideas.

Develop creative teams to work on ideas. When putting teams together, pay special attention to their composition. Placing people with a diversity of perspectives and backgrounds together is a good way of promoting creativity, provided there is mutual respect for opinions and there is no bullying. To maximise creativity in your organisation, make an effort to know your staff; not only their skills and competencies, but also their attitudes, problem-solving styles and what drives them. Give your staff enough space to be creative and look at new areas of possible business opportunities.

When Walt Disney reconceptualised the amusement park in America in the 1940s and 50s, he refused to conform to existing norms, and dared to challenge how things were, and to explore what they could be. He had a dream and he followed that dream. Disneyland in Florida remains one of the most popular theme parks in the world and the Disney empire lives on, long after Walt's death in 1966.

Renowned American motivational speaker, author and television personality, Les Brown, encourages people to stretch outside their comfort zones, and thus expand their consciousness to strive and achieve. Les himself had a first-hand understanding of this, growing up with little education or financial means in America and later rising to greatness and wealth.

Creativity is not only about inventing something totally new, it is about making new connections: taking a concept and exploring the many ways in which it can be tested, implemented or tried. The challenge is to embrace new possibilities and not become harnessed by daily routines. The creative spirit will need to be embedded into the company's culture, which in itself is not an easy task.

Key points:
- ✓ *Try to offer something different from that offered by your competitors.*
- ✓ *Don't accept perceived limitations on your creativity.*
- ✓ *Nurture the creativity of your staff.*

4 Decision-making

Good decision-making is an essential skill for entrepreneurs. If you are able to make timely and well-considered decisions, then you can lead your team to spectacular and well-deserved success. Some problems and decisions are challenging, and require a lot of thought, emotion and research. Making wrong decisions can be extremely costly and painful.

At the age of twenty-three, Richard Farleigh, a private investor, took the decision to leave the academic life, although he had been offered a scholarship to pursue a PhD at Princeton University in America. Today, Farleigh, who grew up in a foster home in Australia, is a multi-millionaire who has helped over seventy companies with investments and advice. Entrepreneurs often make decisions that others regard as too risky.

There is no magic in making right decisions. Often it is based on your experience, gut feelings and analysis. A number of tools have been developed to assist in the decision-making process but how well they work depends on the quality of the process and the cognitive abilities of those participating. There can be no substitute for sharing the process with people on whom the outcome will have an impact. Often these people are closer to the situation and may have their ears to the ground in a way that you, as the manager, are unable to do.

When making important decisions consider the following factors:

1. What exactly do you have to decide?

2. What is the objective of the decision and when does it have to be made?
3. What background information do you have?
4. Where can you obtain more information?
5. Who is involved – what are their personalities, stakeholding, power and influence?
6. Who can help you? (Include impartial third parties, experts and friends.)
7. Do you have any personal biases or prejudices?
8. What are your choices? (Potential decisions available to you)
9. What would be the ideal outcome and how will the decision impact on the relevant parties?
10. What is the worst-case scenario of each decision?
11. What questions could arise from each decision?

Once you have made a decision and communicated it to the relevant people, be prepared to measure their reaction and to learn from the process. Observe how it could be improved and incorporate any lessons in future decision-making.

The concept of brainstorming (idea generation) is useful if you decide to go for a consultative style where ideas are gathered from those concerned and the decision made by a process of elimination.

Some decisions may not suit idea generation and in this regard there are other styles such as the cost/benefit analysis where you simply add up the value of the benefits of a course of action, and subtract the costs associated with it. It is not always simple to do as assumptions have to be made and the quality and bases for those assumptions are often difficult to predict.

Forcefield Analysis is a technique used to understand the pressures for and against change. It helps you to weigh the importance of these factors, and decide whether the change is worth implementing. There is an abundance of websites that present this and other decision-making tools with illustrations as to how they are used. (Simply enter 'decision-making tools' in your web browser.)

Sharing your decisions and giving your staff a stake where possible is good practice. Staff will be more supportive of a decision when they believe it is partly theirs.

Key points:
✓ *Making wrong decisions can be painful, so take time to make them.*
✓ *Gather relevant information before making big decisions.*
✓ *Communicate your decisions to the relevant people; do not let them find out on the grapevine.*

5 E-principles

In this section there are a number of relevant principles in business that have been termed E-principles, as they all commence with the letter E. They are key to operating a successful business.

1. *Economy* is the careful management of resources to avoid waste and unnecessary spending. In business it is vital you take all possible steps to avoid waste and ensure you make savings. For example: If you do not train your staff and they consistently make mistakes, this can impact adversely on your operation. It is never too early to start thinking about ways to maximise production and reduce waste.

2. *Economies of scale* – Think about how to produce larger quantities of your particular product or service, thus reducing unit costs and overheads. For example: You could negotiate longer-term contracts and obtain better prices from a supplier if you buy your raw materials in bulk. As a result of this you could also purchase an additional piece of machinery and employ an additional worker whose costs in effect would not represent a significant increase in your fixed costs. The cost of the machinery would be realised over time and, in terms of the worker, you would only be paying his/her remuneration and associated costs. The cost of the overheads would not increase correspondingly.

3. *Economies of scope* – Think of ways to offer a wider range of products or services using the

same resources. For example, you may have decided to operate a chain of restaurants. If you should decide to enter the market for frozen foods, using the facilities at your restaurant you will be able to benefit from economies of scope as you will be using the same facilities to produce varying products. You will therefore find that the unit costs of your products fall as your operating expenses are shared.

4. *Efficiency* – Examine ways of improving your operations; for example, how can you reduce the waiting time for your clients, and can there be ways of speeding up the service in your production process? Do you have or engage adequate technology to enhance your business? When Ricardo Semler, owner of a Brazilian company which manufactures marine pumps, dishwashers and related products found that his processes were too 'complex' (e.g. using complex ordering forms added unnecessary work for sales people etc.), he restructured Semco. This move repositioned the company in a positive manner, eliminating waste and creating opportunities. Today, Semco has a solid reputation and is regarded as one of Latin America's fastest-growing companies.

5. *Effectiveness* – Ask yourself: Are customers satisfied with your products and services? Do they do what they purport to do? Are you doing the right things (not just doing things!) to enhance your business? Are you sacrificing quality for quantity?

6. *Environment* – Consider: is your operation damaging the environment? For example, can you reduce your use of non-recyclable materials? Anita Roddick, founder of The Body Shop, was well known for her strong belief in protecting the environment. Her company was one of the first to sell products not tested on animals. Yet The Body Shop is said to be among the top thirty worldwide brands serving several million customers per day in over fifty countries.

7. *Ethics* – Are you fair in the various relationships you sustain? Do you keep your promises; and are you honest in what you say? Business ethics is about your relationship with your employees: how you communicate with them, relate to them and the sort of work environment you create for them. It is about empathy and the need to help your employees to work better. Ethics is also about how you feel about what you are doing – are you true to yourself? Do you feel that you are doing your best to make the venture a success and not merely relying on employees? Maria Kempinska gave us food for thought in this area when she said: 'the secret is to know what you are there for – and then to do what you do extremely well.' Kempinska founded Jongleurs Club in 1983, and later sold it for millions of pounds.

8. *Equal Opportunity* – A number of considerations are relevant in this regard. Do you treat people of varying backgrounds fairly? Do you consider adapting your workspaces for disabled workers?

Do you hire staff from different cultures? When you advertise your vacancies do you actively encourage people from different orientations to apply? How are people promoted in your company? Do women have the same opportunities as men? Do your rewards match performance, irrespective of people's differences?

The foregoing considerations should be uppermost in your mind if you are keen to excel with integrity. The list is not exhaustive; indeed any behaviour that allows you to enhance your operation in a holistic, honest way should be considered.

Key points:
- ✓ *There is no need to be lean and mean; effectiveness and good sense are usually enough.*
- ✓ *Be aware of how you treat people, within and outside of your organization.*

6 *Faith*

You must believe in what you do. Be positive and passionate about it and accompany your faith by works. When things seem tough, you must stick with it and have faith in yourself and your business. Life is packed with sticks and stones, valleys and mountains but we survive anyway. If you have a good idea and the appropriate skills, and you have done the necessary groundwork, stick with it. Do not get discouraged and give up because, at the end of a tunnel, there is usually light.

Dr John Gray, the noted American psychologist and best-selling author, writes: 'What we believe is what we create'. Do you believe you can have a successful business?

If you are faced with negativity, use it as fuel to drive you to work harder to succeed. When you are faithful you exercise patience. The first few years may not yield any profits but as long as you feel you are moving forward you must remain focused. It is easy to let impatience overcome you, and waiting to achieve your goals can be very frustrating.

In order to believe in something, you must know what that thing is. Define it; know what your goals are; have a clear vision. Know what you are about and ensure those who work with you also understand your mission.

Faith in your business and what you are doing is important and will help keep you focused and patient. However, it is also important not to have blind faith. You must be able to recognise when the horse is dead and stop flogging it. Do not waste your energy trying to revive a project at all costs because you may end up with nothing but costs. If it is not going where you want it to go, and you cannot see a glimmer of light, give it up. How long you should keep going is up to you. It would be reasonable to say that if you have had three years of negative growth then it may be time to change focus.

Having faith in your business is not an automatic ability. For this to occur you must believe in your ability to make it happen. If you don't, it could lead to a self-fulfilling prophecy and in effect you will not be able to make it happen. When the recession hit and our funding dried up at ACT, it was mere faith coupled with endurance and hard work that enabled the company to keep afloat. It was the belief that things would get better and the belief in ourselves as an organisation that helped us to weather the storm. We held it together, balancing all the variables and continuing our marketing activities, not panicking but believing that we could do it despite all the challenges.

You must do your best to make it work and believe in your efforts. Put in the work necessary to realise your dream. You have to be confident that you have put the mechanisms in place and selected the right people to help make it happen.

Recruitment and selection are processes that must be done carefully. In some cultures it is advantageous to have family and friends at the initial stage and sometimes beyond. Those closest to you may have a stronger commitment to the company than the average employee. They are likely to work overtime without remuneration as they regard themselves as direct, short, medium and long-term beneficiaries. In addition, they may be more loyal to you.

When you are able, it is also a good idea to help your family to set up in business themselves if they are so inclined. This is what James Caan, Pakistani-born multimillionaire investor did. In these instances you will often need to build capacity, ensuring that family members are able to manage the business well. James himself had made the decision not to join the family business as was expected, but instead to launch his own bid to enter the business world via different channels.

In some cultures, hiring family and friends can be a recipe for chaos. Doing so may make it more difficult to fire them; others in the organisation may see the hiring as nepotism (especially if the family member lacks the appropriate experience or training); and family disagreements may be brought into the workplace. Be prepared to manage these events when they occur and do not allow them to fester.

Understand your culture and your particular situation and know what works for you.

Key points:
- ✓ *If you don't believe it, you won't make it happen.*
- ✓ *Faith alone won't do; you have to work hard.*
- ✓ *Recognise when the idea is dead and if it is, bury it!*

7 Globalisation

Think big! Gone are the days when people in business were confined to a small area, selling their goods and services to a local market. These days the opportunities are endless. For example, if you are selling goods that can be used in China, don't worry about not being able to speak Chinese. China's population exceeds one billion; you cannot afford to ignore that opportunity.

Globalisation is a business philosophy based on the belief that the world is becoming more standardised – needs and wants are becoming less distinct across nations. It means therefore that there is a greater level of connection and interdependence among people.

There are several driving forces contributing to the growth of international business nowadays, for example: the creation of new markets, the growth in communication media, the consistency of technology across national and cultural boundaries, and the deregulation of international capital markets.

People across the world are more connected to each other than ever before; information flows more quickly and the methods of collecting payments are much more varied. With increased trade liberalization treaties and the creation of economic blocs, there are real opportunities for international trade. Competition in transportation media such as air travel allows more frequent air flights, and goods and services produced in one part of the world are almost instantly available in others. All these factors drive globalisation, and businesspeople should consider the possibilities if they are going to compete and stay afloat in the increasingly competitive global trade arena.

The internet is making it possible to communicate with people all over the world as it doesn't recognise geopolitical and cultural borders. As with most things, the internet has its dangers and unfortunately fraudsters are also cashing in on technology. Be prudent and recognise there are unscrupulous people in every corner of the world who seek opportunities to prey on others. So while this massive growth in technology can be an opportunity, be aware of its potential threats. In general, the benefits of using the internet to access information on suppliers, manufactures, customers and potential customers, networking opportunities etc, generally outweigh the threats, provided the necessary care is taken when transacting business online.

Globalization is no longer an option but a strategic advantage for most businesses. The internet makes it possible to have a round-the-clock marketplace and offers more flexibility than was previously possible. There is always somewhere in the world where people are awake; the internet makes it possible for trade to take place even when business owners are asleep. The potential for cross-border trade has grown tremendously and the idea of wealth creation is now a real possibility.

Opening your doors to the opportunities makes perfect sense. Let's take the case of a small Caribbean farmer who is successfully exporting to the UK. The benefits to be derived for him are:

- Increased sales – resulting from a bigger market.

- Higher profits – advantageous exchange rates resulting in the possibility of charging more for goods.
- Diversified markets – resulting in the ability to develop new products to serve varying customer tastes.
- Less reliance on domestic markets – local competition can be particularly stiff.
- New opportunities to learn and develop – competing in the international arena involves different skills and competencies.
- The opportunity to develop international networks, which in turn opens doors in various other directions.
- The ability to negotiate better prices on a wider scale and interface with larger business customers who may themselves be established globally.

When trading online, ensure you have a website that does justice to your organisation. If your company can benefit from a shopping-cart website, then get one. In considering sites as partners or affiliates, don't forget professional organisations and associations, especially when you market services or business products. Try trading or paying for links with other small or middle-sized e-commerce marketers.

Ensure your site is customer-friendly. Buyers won't want to wade through faulty or overloaded websites or ones that are difficult to navigate. Graphics and Flash make your site look cool, but they can also slow down the loading process causing customers to click away to sites quicker to load.

Ensure that once customers decide to trade with your company online you are able to deliver. Delivery means that you have the systems at the office to receive orders, contact customers if necessary, log information and carry out all complementary processes to ensure the customer is served in a timely, effective way. Ensure your staff is well-trained in using the systems and also in customer service. Make sure your IT systems are up to date and adequate to cope with large orders. If you fail to address all these areas, you risk choking on your own success!

Key points:
- ✓ *Customers are not only living in your region; widen your target area!*
- ✓ *Make use of information technology as much as possible.*
- ✓ *Ensure that your systems can cope when your company starts to grow.*

8 *Honesty*

Honesty does not dictate you should 'reveal all'. Be honest in your dealings with others; do not intentionally mislead or lie. In your negotiations, strive for win-win situations where both parties feel they benefit from any ensuing deal. Partnerships deemed to be unfair to one party are doomed to fail. A partner who feels 'robbed' by the other often has little loyalty and is vulnerable to poaching by competitors. In addition, the 'bad-mouthing' and ill-feeling that can fester will render serious injury to your company's reputation.

It is also important to be honest with your employees. Do not treat them as if they have no intelligence. Treat them with respect, and share decision-making with them. In this way they will be accountable and take responsibility for their actions. Do not make promises that you have no intention or ability to keep. If you are bent on being dishonest you will soon be found out and you will lose credibility. Credibility is important if you want to build loyalty. Loyalty is important if you want to be ahead or simply keep up with the competition. You must keep up with the competition or you will simply be overtaken. If you are overtaken, your business may die prematurely and the undertakers will move in.

Honesty and integrity are closely linked. Keep your reputation in place as far as possible. This is important not only to you but to your employees who like to know they are working for a reputable employer. A strong reputation may also protect you from attempts by your competitors to discredit you to their own advantage.

There are situations that can call your integrity into question, even if you are honest in your intentions. This can arise, for example, in the case of accepting or giving gifts to clients and key stakeholders. Bribery comes in different forms and you must ensure that your organisation cannot be accused of accepting any form of bribe. If you must accept gifts do have a policy in place and limit these to special occasions when it is customary to give or accept them. Avoid any situation that makes it appear that you have accepted favours in the context of your business. Avoid offering or accepting monetary gifts. You need not sacrifice your hospitality, but be ever mindful of how things can be interpreted and, as far as is possible, avoid hospitality that can be reasonably regarded as personal rewards.

Commit your organisation to fair and honest competition and always endeavour to engage in straightforward business transactions. Be aware of antitrust and competition laws, for example those that prohibit price fixing and supplier boycott, mis-representation of competitors and sniping.

Also important is the need to balance honesty with wisdom. It is honest to tell all, but wise to keep some things to yourself, if they will not help your situation. For example, in making a presentation about your company, do not say: 'we have not made any money in the last couple of years but we hope to change that in the future'. If this information is necessary, say instead: 'our revenue in recent years has been below targeted levels, but we expect to move closer to our goals during the current year'. In this way you are being honest but economical with the truth. This is wisdom. You don't want to shoot yourself in the foot; people are reluctant to do business with a company that is perceived as failing. Use positive language, and balance honesty with wisdom.

Being honest is also a relationship that you should have with yourself. Sir Richard Branson is respected both nationally and internationally as an accomplished entrepreneur. However, along with his large number of extremely successful business ventures, he has had a number of projects that have failed. One of his particular strengths as an entrepreneur is his ability to recognise when to call the day on a particular venture. In not being afraid of admitting his mistakes, Richard Branson is a man who is honest with himself.

Key points:
- ✓ *Being honest is important; wisdom is invaluable.*
- ✓ *Always aim for win-win situations.*
- ✓ *Build and protect your reputation.*

9 Invoicing

Getting your invoicing system and payment terms right can be key to a healthy cash-flow. If everyone understands how much they need to pay and when they must settle, they are more likely to pay on time.

Ensuring customers pay their bills on time can be difficult. It's a serious issue – late or non-payment of debts can cause cash-flow problems – and could even force you out of business. In outlining his rules for success, Cypriot retail magnate Theo Paphitis listed his number one rule as 'Cash is All'. He likened a lack of cash-flow to a fatal heart attack – instant death.

It is good for your cash-flow if you can get your customers to pay in full in advance. If this is not possible, try to get a deposit, which could be calculated to meet the initial costs of fulfilling an order or service.

If a customer will only deal with you by paying invoices in arrears, take the necessary steps to ensure you get paid, and on time. Make sure you have an effective invoicing system. The invoicing process can become complicated, especially when receiving payments in instalments. As a minimum, use an Excel spreadsheet with appropriately headed columns and formulae to ensure payments are requested and collected when due. Implement quality controls to check outstanding monies are tracked and collected. Some creditors will not pay if the invoice is over six months overdue so do dispatch invoices quickly.

If customers delay their payments, investigate the reasons behind their actions. Check if there are any complaints or disagreements relating to your product or service. Remember, some companies and individuals fail to pay on time because they themselves are experiencing cash-flow problems. In extreme instances you may need to pursue legal action, but in doing so weigh up the costs of engaging in a lawsuit and running your business. You will find that in some cases it is cheaper to write off the debt and focus on your business. Learn any lessons to be learnt and ensure you take steps to reduce the risk of non-payment.

Before transacting business with customers, it is necessary to set out clear terms and conditions, including:

- Price.
- Arrangements for delivery.
- Payment terms – if you don't agree a credit period with your customers, thirty days is usually acceptable.
- Quality.
- The right to charge interest on late payments and claim compensation for debt recovery costs – you may need to boost your resources in order to chase late payments effectively.

Vetting your customers is one way of protecting yourself against non-payment. When you are about to secure a deal, it can be tempting to skip vetting the customer beforehand. However, extending credit in this way can leave you exposed to the risk of not being paid. Conducting credit checks on new and existing customers can reduce your vulnerability. Ensure that you obtain information from your new customers including:

- Full name of the customer's business and whether it trades under a different name.
- Registration number, charity number or other number as appropriate.
- How much credit is being requested.
- Full contact details of the person responsible for payment queries.
- Delivery and invoice address if different.
- Bank account details.
- At least two trade references.
- Request for consent to obtain bank and credit
- references.
- Details of who owns – and who runs – the business.

It is particularly important to collect monies owed to you because inevitably you will waste some money in the early stages. This comes in many forms – preparing literature that is never used, advertising that yields no returns, travel to meetings that are a waste of time, taking out contracts for services that were ineffective or unnecessary, buying things for the office that are never used, buying too much of any one item, spoilage, and the list goes on.

Maintaining an effective invoicing system is essential in any business. Ensure that you collect all that is due to you; after all, being financially sound is a key aspiration of all businesses.

Key points:
- ✓ *Collect your money; that's the whole point of your business.*
- ✓ *Put in place a good financial system to keep track of your invoices.*
- ✓ *Vet your customers before extending credit and, if that is not possible, limit your liability by collecting payments in instalments.*

10 Jargon

In business, you should familiarise yourself with the basic jargon used in your industry. You will often attend meetings and people will be discussing issues relating to your sector. You may find it difficult to appreciate the discussion or to contribute if you do not know the relevant jargon. Perception is reality in a given moment. If others perceive you to be lacking in knowledge they may think you are unintelligent and fail to treat you with the respect you deserve.

Every industry has its set of words used. In addition, there are some acronyms in management that are bandied about irrespective of the industry in question, e.g. SWOT (Strengths, Weaknesses, Opportunities and Threats), USP (Unique Selling Proposition) and KPIs (Key Performance Indicators). The use of business jargon is common and can often cause confusion and misunderstanding. Some people habitually use buzz-words, taking for granted that everyone understands them.

Your particular industry will have some jargon and this should be part of your vocabulary if you wish to join in as an equal. If in your formal presentations you decide to use cultural jargon do ensure you are fully conversant with its meaning and relevance. In your one-to-one conversations keep jargon to a minimum but be prepared to hear and react to it.

In your business dealings, try to avoid cultural jargon which has no meaning to your audience. Furthermore, different nations utilise different jargon to denote different meanings. You can be on dangerous ground if you try to be funny using jargon or phrases that in your culture seem harmless. When in doubt, do not make jokes.

You need to consider the use of language and general communication skills in general management. Unless you are running a boot camp, mind your manners. People do not like to be shouted at or talked down to. If you embrace this behaviour you will watch your best workers leave, perhaps poached by the very competitors that they helped you to beat in the past. In your written communication you need to remain professional. Do not write your emails or letters as if you were sending a text to your friend, even if the official letter is being written to your friend. For example, 'you are' is spelt y-o-u a-r-e; not u r. Think of other organisations as a group of people with diverse backgrounds and orientations, many of whom will not understand your text language and many more who will not appreciate it. If you wish to be treated professionally, you need to operate professionally.

Ensure your use of language is professional and earns the respect of those around you. It is pointless using jargon or complicated words if the other party misses the meaning. If you insist on punctuating your sentences with technical language you are effectively putting up a barrier and this can lead to mixed messages between yourself and others. In addition it makes it difficult for people to understand instructions and this in turn may impact adversely on their performance.

Entrepreneurs cannot afford to miscommunicate their messages. They need to be able to transmit and receive information from their staff quickly and effectively.

They should be aware that some people are embarrassed to ask the meaning of words and this can result in a lack of understanding and subsequent breakdown of communication. Ensure your instructions are clear and make yourself available for workers to seek clarification if required. Ensure you build credibility so that workers have faith in your message. Do not promise what you cannot deliver and do not deliver what you cannot afford. Keep in mind that your workers, network partners and other stakeholders come from varying backgrounds and have different experiences that determine the meanings they assign to words.

Be careful not to block out information you are not comfortable with. Managers often analyse problems based on their frame of reference. Poor communication can be the root cause of low morale, resistance to change, conflict, grievance, low productivity and reduced profits.

Be sure to listen. Too often managers fail to allocate time to listening, citing their busy schedule. If you have no time to listen to others, one day you will find that all you have is time and no one to listen to you. A day has twenty-four hours; make time for your most important assets – your staff.

Key points:
- ✓ *Learn relevant jargon but don't use it unnecessarily.*
- ✓ *Enhance your communication by steering clear of jargon.*
- ✓ *Use respectful language when dealing with people.*

11 *Kaizen*

In a nutshell, Kaizen is a Japanese word, which means *continuous improvement*. It aims to teach people how to perform to high standards, not necessarily by working harder, but by improving efficiency and effectiveness and eliminating waste. Once a winning formula has been identified it is standardised until an improved way is found.

Everyone in the organisation is involved – the managing director, the marketing manager, the cleaner, as well as external stakeholders where necessary. Those directly involved in production activities are best positioned to identify lean processes that bring about improvements. The sharing of knowledge is more effective when everyone is involved and a culture of continuous improvement is fostered. If wasteful activities are removed, employees are able to work smarter and are able to spend more time in processes that create value for customers.

It doesn't have to be a big change; it could simply be a change in a small part of the process. For example, in a small retail operation the use of a simple system to record information for the manager about stock levels could enhance responsiveness, ensuring that the items are ordered before current stock is depleted. The principle of Kaizen assumes the following:

1. *Personal discipline* – Staff must be able to recognise that they have targets to meet and be able to work on their own to achieve those

targets. They must be empowered and made accountable for their work, not constantly hounded.

2. *Teamwork* – Teams are often lost in some organisations. They fail to recognise that the term 'team' may not be used but nonetheless their employees are still working as a team. A team has certain characteristics and goes through stages – forming, storming, norming, performing and adjourning. Unlike a group, a team works together towards a specific, well-defined, timed goal.

3. *Improved morale* – Staff morale is key to effectiveness. There are various ways of boosting morale; key among them are: respect for staff, recognition for their work, participation and involvement and team-building efforts. Once remuneration is at acceptable levels, it has little or no bearing on morale. People are motivated by the way they are treated and the way they are made to feel in the workplace.

4. *Quality circles* – These are constituted by a group of workers who meet to discuss workplace improvement, and present their ideas to decisionmakers. These are meant to improve staff performance, increase a sense of ownership, motivate staff and boost morale.

5. *Suggestions for improvement* – These suggestions can come from any stakeholder of the organisation. Businesses should be careful not to overlook the opinions of people on the *frontline* who have firsthand knowledge of issues

and who can provide valuable insight into possible incremental improvements that will go a long way to satisfying customer needs and boost sales.

If an organisation is to continuously grow in an increasingly competitive marketplace, the principle of Kaizen has a key role to play. The achievement of big goals is usually the result of smaller combined efforts. The attention to detail will reduce or eliminate waste, get rid of pointless activity, improve efficiency and effectiveness and render your organisation more professional and profitable overall.

Key points:
- ✓ *Aim to continuously improve existing operations.*
- ✓ *Involve everyone in the drive for improvement.*
- ✓ *Recognise small efforts, not only the big ones!*

12 *Leadership*

Leadership is about working with people, accepting responsibility, understanding people, motivating, developing and encouraging. It is also about knowing when to stand back and allow others to take the lead, for a good leader is also a follower. A good leader is not threatened by the growth and development of his staff; indeed he or she is encouraged by it. He or she enjoys empowering people and watching them grow; and he knows when and what to delegate. It is said that entrepreneurs are born with deep, innate personal characteristics that allow them to spot opportunities, influence people and make things happen. However, there are many qualities that can be learned or developed. For example, some entrepreneurs are good leaders but not good managers. They may have the drive and determination to succeed but lack the skills to motivate people. In order to be successful over the long term it is vital that they learn how to work with people and motivate their team.

Leaders are people who are able to think and act spontaneously and respond to unprogrammed, emergent situations and circumstances. They set out to influence the actions, beliefs and feelings of others. Not all managers are leaders; and not all leaders are managers. In your quest to run a successful enterprise, you must display leadership qualities, even if you are not a born leader.

To be a successful leader who people will follow, you must inspire confidence in others in your ability to lead. People want to know that they will not be led into a brick wall. They want to belong to an enterprise that is taking them somewhere: building on their careers and generating hope for the future. People often resist change but they will remain with you if they are convinced you have the intelligence, stamina, competence, skills, drive, courage and confidence to lead the organisation, motivating people and driving growth. They want to know you will lead from the front and you will be strong enough to interface with *dragons* in the industry who often swoop down on vulnerable organisations in order to protect their turf.

Good leaders help to pick up the pieces when things go wrong; they learn lessons and share knowledge. They are not quick to criticise and knock down; instead they build up and nurture. Naturally, there will be times when a leader has to be assertive, even dictatorial, but never tyrannical or arrogant. In his book, *The Seven Day Weekend,* Brazilian entrepreneur, Ricardo Semler, reveals that in his company, Semco, they 'want people to self-manage as intensely as possible, leaving leadership to those whose talent resides in helping others get where they want to go'. Semco is a well-known, maverick organisation that has operated successfully in Brazil for many years.

Leaders need to lead and allow others to get on with tasks, while providing the necessary guidance and structure where necessary. The foundation of excellent leadership is honourable character and devoted service to the organisation. Your employees view your leadership as everything you do that impacts on the organisation's objectives and their well-being.

Respected leaders are judged on their character, knowledge and understanding of the job, their interactions with people, their ability to motivate and direct, and the results achieved. Semler goes on to say: 'It is important to keep egos under control'. People with a high opinion of themselves can clash with others unduly; this is unhelpful in a work environment.

Good leaders help their employees understand the company's mission, vision and goals and show them how they fit and contribute to the business objectives. Sharing information with employees on the progress of the company inspires employees and is good practice.

People want to be guided by those they respect who have a clear sense of direction. There is nothing worse than frustrating good employees by sending mixed messages, having no unity of command or by blurring the boundaries between the professional and the personal. It is difficult, if not impossible, to achieve an ever-moving objective.

A good leader cultivates a healthy climate in the workplace, providing direction, sharing rewards, offering incentives, building teams and generating hope and confidence in the future – especially in times of uncertainty. In a nutshell, those who own and run businesses are more likely to succeed if they are:

1. *Motivated* – Clear on what their motivations are – money, fame, or the desire to make a difference to the lives of people. They are clear on what their defining success factors are and they are keen to get going. For the true entrepreneur, money is merely the reward, while the ability to

succeed, particularly in challenging circumstances, is the motivation.

2. *Self-confident* – Able to lead from the front and
   remain calm in difficult and discouraging
   circumstances. Self-confidence allows the
   entrepreneur to listen without being easily
   swayed or intimidated. Self-confidence comes
   from thorough planning, which reduces
   uncertainty and the level of risk. It also comes
   from expertise.

3. *Multi-skilled* – Able to develop a product, market
   it and collect payment. They are also able to
   carry out mundane back office tasks when
   necessary to ensure their dreams become reality.

4. *Innovative and creative* – Able to identify
   windows of opportunity and carve out new
   niches in the marketplace, often invisible to
   others. Creativity drives the development of new
   products and services, or ways of conducting
   business. It is the spark that ignites innovation
   and improvement, continuous learning, probing
   and personal growth.

5. *Results-orientated* – Able to set goals and targets
   and derive pleasure from achieving them. The
   entrepreneur will not rest until he achieves a
   positive outcome.

6. *Risk takers* – Willing to take measured risks to
   drive their ideas. They take risks that others find
   rather daunting and often incredible. They have a
   drive, seemingly a hunger to try risky ventures,
   which when successful pay bigger dividends.

Unfortunately, when things go wrong their losses can be just as huge.

7. *Committed and dedicated* – Possess dogged determination, are hardworking, energetic and focused. Dedication motivates entrepreneurs to work long hours, especially at the start, to get the venture off the ground. Determination – a strong desire to achieve success – demonstrates itself in persistence and the ability to bounce back after encountering challenges.

8. *Flexible* – Able to move quickly in response to changing market needs. They follow their dreams while being mindful of market realities. They are able to adapt to their customers' changing needs and to changing environmental factors.

9. *Leaders* – Able to lead from the front and inspire staff to share the vision and ultimately accomplish set goals. They inspire confidence (even when deep down they are unsure of the outcomes) and they allow their workers to lead when necessary.

10. *Passionate* – Believe strongly in the idea and able to convince others to 'see' their vision. Most people believe in their own dreams but entrepreneurs take it further; they are convinced that theirs is great and they do everything in their power to prove it.

Key points:
- ✓ *Leaders lead from the front and lead by example.*
- ✓ *Leaders share information and allow employees to do their work.*
- ✓ *Motivating and developing people are key roles of good leaders.*

13 Marketing

Marketing is a key role in any business enterprise. You can sell a bad product if you know how to market it (but we advise you don't!). On the other hand, you can watch the best product die in your hands if you cannot attract an appropriate market.

Marketing refers to the wide range of activities involved in making sure you are continuing to meet the wants and needs of your customers and getting value in return.

Marketing activities include market research to ascertain, for example, what groups of potential customers exist, what their needs are, which of those needs you can meet and how you should meet them. It also involves analysing the competition, positioning your new product or service, finding your niche, pricing and promoting your products and services.

Deborah Meaden, noted British marketer, is a keen believer in research. Deborah made her millions in the leisure industry and currently devotes herself to sourcing investment opportunities. She advises: 'If you are marketing an item, you have to find out who your customers are, where they are and why they would want to buy your product.'

Do not take for granted that your product will be snapped up off the shelves without the necessary groundwork. You must have a marketing plan and take note of the seven Ps of marketing:

1. *Product* – Ensure the features and benefits of your product or service are well established and

that they suit the specifications your customers (and potential customers) demand. Products go through a number of phases, called a life cycle:

   i) Introduction – product is new to the market;

   ii) Growth – market share increases and competition appears;

   iii) Maturity – strong competition abounds and market share diminishes and

   iv) Decline – product loses its appeal and may have to be replaced. Customers needs constantly change; it would be a mistake to keep your product or service static in such an environment.

2. *Price* – There are several considerations in setting your price but ultimately the price you set will depend greatly on the industry you are in and your target market. Some people are willing to pay high prices for higher quality, either real or perceived. If your prices are too low you could be losing money and risk the viability and image of the business. In addition, you may make yourself a few enemies as your competitors will not be happy with you for undercutting their prices. If your prices are too high in the introductory stage of your product lifecycle you may find it difficult to penetrate the market. Find the right balance between price, quality and competitiveness and you will have found a winning formula.

3. *Promotion* – Allocate resources for creating awareness about your product. As a new business, you will need to watch your advertising choices and costs but do choose appropriate

media for getting the message out to customers. Sell the benefits rather than the features – what it can do for the buyer, how it solves a problem etc. Be aware of the various means of promoting your product or service. Do take advantage of cheaper forms of promoting your business such as word of mouth, networking and internet advertising.

4. *Place* – choose your distribution channels in accordance with your customer habits. For example, how much can you expect to make if you are selling your product online and your customer base is concentrated in an area known to have little access to computers? Effective distribution decisions will ensure that your product is available for your target market once a demand for it has been established. If you are using third parties to distribute your product or service, choose your distributors carefully. Check references to ensure that they are reliable and have optimum customer service ethics. Maintain positive relationships with them and ensure that they understand the need to communicate with you constantly, especially if they are unable to satisfy a customer.

5. *People* – People are your most important assets and are undoubtedly the most important element of any service. Unlike machines they are able to alter what they can offer to meet the individual needs of the consumer. With the appropriate attitude, skills and appearance people can work wonders for your business. Ensure they are well trained and motivated and treat them well. There

is no point training your staff and then not paying them well and offering incentives. If this is allowed to happen you may lose your best workers to the competition and worst of all, you will have helped to train them!

6. *Process* – Process takes into consideration how the customer experiences what an organisation is offering. It is something that your customer participates in at different points in time. For example, if you are offering courses and a client walks into your company, the process begins with a greeting, followed by information exchange, offer of refreshments (if appropriate), completion of relevant paperwork, an allocation of dates, a follow-up call, the course itself, examination and qualification. Throughout the process, information should be clear and correct and the progress should be timely. Make it easy to do business with your company; customers do not enjoy participating in cumbersome, difficult processes when spending their money.

7. *Physical evidence* – Show the clients what your product or service can do for them. If you have testimonials or demonstrations or a track record, ensure these are accessible and that people can see them. Potential customers, especially those who are undecided, can be convinced to buy your service if you give them a bit of encouragement through real evidence. Think in terms of everything that the customer sees from the first moment of contact with your organisation all the way through the purchasing process. The

physical evidence also refers to the way your product or service appears from the outside, the appearance and decorum of your staff, your offices, waiting rooms, marketing materials, correspondence and every single visual element of your company. Every aspect of your company affects your customers' confidence and how they trade with you.

Being able to find and penetrate new and existing markets for your product or service is fundamental. You fail to do this and the business will struggle to maintain and grow its market share.

Key points:
- ✓ *A good product or service without marketing will not sell.*
- ✓ *It is important to identify your market preferably a niche, which you can service effectively.*
- ✓ *Market research provides valuable information; do it!*

14 Networking

Networking involves interacting with others for assistance and support. When you network for business purposes you have opportunities to:

- meet in organised and informal environments to share information relevant to a field of interest.
- receive news bulletins and invitations to events of general interest, e.g. exhibitions and lectures by prominent businesspeople or industry experts.
- participate in debates on topics relevant to your industry or field of business.
- contribute to or participate in surveys or research in your field or business sector.
- meet customers, competitors, suppliers and service providers who are all looking for similar benefits and to widen their contact base.
- gain from the experiences of other businesses and share new ideas on a variety of subjects including: training and recruitment, talent management, new products and markets, industry developments, industry laws and regulation.

Networking has many benefits. For a start-up or small business, it can provide a lifeline of support and business generation. It also helps you improve your business performance, products and staff skills, and provides opportunities for you to develop your knowledge and skills. There are also other advantages:

- Participating in benchmarking opportunities helps you identify areas where you can improve your business performance.
- Organisations can benefit from economies of scale by involving employees in joint skills development programmes in your business sector.
- Businesses can raise their profile and build their brand by becoming an established and regular networking member.
- Individuals meet new people and build mutually beneficial business relationships.
- There are opportunities to expand your markets by generating new business contacts with potential customers, suppliers and partners.
- The opportunity to compare and discuss issues of common interest, e.g. legal and regulatory developments, staff retention, supplier networks, customer service and computerization.
- Network partners can develop and share ideas, innovation and knowledge of best practice.

Les Brown, the noted American professional speaker and author, offers some advice in his motivational literature when he says: 'find some good company'. He encourages people to seek assistance where necessary and avoid isolation, especially in hard times. Being part of a network is a valuable resource centre when the road becomes lonely.

The extent to which you benefit will depend on the events and services the network partnership offers and how actively you become involved. Some leaders are reluctant to seek advice or obtain help for fear of being embarrassed; they may also feel they are exposing their weakness and a competitor may see an opportunity to take advantage. However, for most businesses, the benefits of taking an active role in a network usually outweigh any potential concerns or reasons not to network.

When choosing a network to join, think of your primary requirements, e.g. market information, training and development opportunities, or expert advice. Aim to balance your needs with the level of participation and involvement you are prepared to commit. You can find networking partners through personal introductions by an existing network member or by contacting the organisation or body they are interested in directly. You could also speak to your local Business Support Centre or Chamber of Commerce, business adviser, e.g. your bank manager, lawyer, accountant or trade association.

In your endeavour to develop networks and establish liaisons, be careful not to raise your expectations too high at networking events. Too often individuals meet and at that moment indicate interest in keeping in touch or taking the business relationship further. However, after the event they totally (or conveniently) forget and you find it difficult to gain access to them or to maintain their interest. One of the attributes of businesspeople is the ability to be tactful. Unfortunately, some people are very good at this but in an unhelpful way. They are often not genuine and have no intention of following through on their momentary promises. This can lead to false expectations and some unfortunate misunderstandings.

This is not to say you should always be sceptical, it is just a fact of which you should be aware.

Sometimes your efforts to establish meaningful liaisons with organisations and key personnel are frustrated. It is important to note that despite what you think about an individual, you should never allow him/her to annoy you to the point where you lose your temper. Do not let them know that you absolutely hate working with them because if you do, you will be feeding their ego and allowing them to manipulate your emotions. When possible, walk away quietly and always remain professional. Do not burn your bridges because you never know when you will need to cross that way again.

In building your networks you should attend events, for example: breakfast meetings, exhibitions, sales presentations and training seminars. Sometimes you will feel that you are wasting your time by attending such events. While this is true, do not underestimate the value of the intelligence you can gather – knowledge of key players, changes in the industry, developments in the marketplace and other key data. You may not attract immediate business opportunities but you could gain ideas for future product development, establish key contacts or get ideas for new business ventures based on what you observed and learnt.

In business it is not good to isolate yourself or get bogged down with day-to-day operations, leaving no time for interacting with people outside your organisation.

Key points:
- ✓ *Make an effort to know people and draw on your contacts where necessary.*
- ✓ *Networking has many benefits; not just financial ones.*
- ✓ *Being informed about your industry is key to business performance; join the appropriate organisations to keep abreast.*

15   Organisational Learning

There are lots of lessons to be learnt in your experience as a businessperson. Whatever you do, learn from your mistakes and try not to make them twice.

Organizational learning encourages, fosters and facilitates learning throughout the organisation and uses this learning to effect improvements. In a learning organisation, knowledge is shared by all and there is a concerted effort to continuously learn new ways of performing and letting go of processes, procedures and other practices that do not promote learning and development.

Forward-thinking companies in pursuit of excellence recognise early on that human resources are their most important assets. Academic study constantly needs updating and so training and skills development must be constant. Learning can take place in various ways and organisations should not worry too much about funding for the training. By applying creativity, common sense, and a small amount of financial investment, organisations can develop their staff using coaching techniques, by negotiating with external consultants or by accessing subsidised training. In this manner they can keep abreast of developments in their industry and the wider community.

Learning organisations thrive on change and are not scared to try new approaches. They train and empower people and have a culture of participation and involvement. They plan, take action and learn from past actions. They adapt to changes in the business environment and ensure that those charged with leading change as well as those involved in the change are enlightened and that they recognise the need for change and their role in it. They reward performance and encourage individual and team development. They encourage double-loop learning whereby individuals can question processes and make suggestions for improvements. Entrepreneurs who have an autocratic management style may feel uncomfortable with this type of learning but they are well advised to allow their team to explore their creativity for the benefit of the organisation.

At ACT we were keen to maintain a professional dress code and saw this as a fundamental part of our image. However, some members of staff struggled with this requirement and eventually presented a petition for change. We eventually struck a compromise and allowed staff to 'dress down' on Fridays. This had no effect on the output but had a positive impact on the staff who were generally very happy with the decision. We had learned, thanks to our open, collaborative management style that we could make changes to our culture without any repercussions.

Today's failure is fodder for tomorrow's success. Learning is achieved not only from one's own actions but also from the actions and omissions of other companies and individuals. When, at the age of twenty-nine, British tycoon, Peter Jones, lost everything, he had to learn quickly. No doubt his employees had to learn quickly too. Being in business involves continuous learning and being able to foresee and react to change. The experience of losing all that had been amassed was invaluable in Peter's entrepreneurial growth and he went on to make millions from the sale of technological items, property and media.

Learning is a process to be nurtured. People have a natural desire to learn and do so more easily in a non-threatening environment where they are free to make mistakes. People fail to learn because of a lack of motivation, fear of failure and lack of interest. Coaching is an effective medium of training, enhancing achievement, fulfilment, performance and development. Coaching inspires, energises and boosts performance. It helps the worker to raise awareness, generate new ideas and foster creativity.

Coaching benefits both employees and managers: employees have improved performance, experience greater enthusiasm and greater job satisfaction; managers improve their skills of communication, delegation, planning and motivation. The organisation also benefits by having a more skilled workforce and managers that demonstrate empathy and good leadership, able to motivate staff and boost organizational growth. Finding the right balance between management, leadership and coaching is a task that the manager has to conquer in order to lead the organisation effectively.

Learning in an organisation is to be proactively developed and nurtured for it is the capacity to learn that enhances the organisation's survival and growth.

Key points:
- ✓ *Foster a culture of continuous learning and information sharing in your organisation.*
- ✓ *People should not feel overly scared of making mistakes.*
- ✓ *Provide opportunities for staff to enhance their personal development.*

16 *People*

People are your most important asset. Your products, structures and style can be copied by competitors. However, no one can copy your unique blend of skilled, motivated personnel. People have tacit knowledge and are central to your company's competitive advantage. Senior management alone cannot take a successful company forward; you need loyal, supportive staff who are willing to go the extra mile to make it happen.

Motivating employees takes an investment. Spend time to develop your staff, empower them and enrich their employment.

As a training organisation, we at ACT encourage our staff to participate in our training programmes and where necessary we fund their places. These programmes do not have to be directly related to their work as we believe that knowledge builds capacity and helps the employees to develop their personal and professional repertoire, which ultimately is good for the company. Allow your staff to be a part of the decision-making process; show them that their opinions are valued. Let them work with autonomy and have meaningful input into operations. Grant them greater levels of accountability and responsibility for their decisions.

Your employees must appreciate the vision and mission of your company and understand its culture. They must share in your company's prosperity and be motivated to push for greater achievements.

There are varying forms of business status that are open to you. For example, you could decide to form a limited company, a partnership or to set up as a sole trader. Whichever form you choose, it is important to have people on board with you. Running a business as a sole trader is fine but it can be very difficult for one person especially in the early stages to manage all the aspects of the business – finance, administration, product development, customer relationship, marketing and sales.

In the early stages finding finance for human resource can be a challenge but in the absence of practical help you can become overwhelmed and burnt out, leaving you with little energy to grow your business. In addition, there are decisions that you will have to make that you would like to remain confidential. These may not be suited even to your most trusted employees and it would be better if someone with a greater stake could brainstorm and analyse them with you. You have to think about this very carefully; consider whether it would be worth giving a stake to another person in order to alleviate the pressures. If you do decide to go down this route, this decision must be made after careful thought. Consider first, what does the person bring to the table (e.g. finance, product development expertise, marketing skills)? Does the person have adequate time to do the work? Is there a synergy between you and the person? What power and influence will they have and what is their motivation for joining the business? Once you are satisfied with this you must have a clear written understanding of the roles and responsibilities and the share ratio (if applicable). It is worth engaging the services of a corporate lawyer to clarify and document the relationship and thus reduce any future problems that may arise.

Ricardo Semler, CEO of Semco, is a keen advocate of empowering people based on trust and participation, with minimal levels of management. He transformed his company from a formal, hierarchical organisation to a much more participative organisation by trusting his employees and eliminating red tape and rules. In his book *Maverick* he reveals that the workers of the company are self-governing and self managing – a truly maverick concept in management, even in the twenty-first century. Semco is one of Brazil's most notable success stories, contributing significant amounts to the country's Gross Domestic Product.

Help your employees to appreciate the need to work as a team. Teamwork is essential for competing in today's global arena where the output of the whole exceeds the sum of its individual parts. By enhancing the synergy within the workplace a healthy atmosphere will be created and higher levels of production will take place.

Retaining and finding the best staff is increasingly difficult. Treating staff well is one way to develop a work environment and culture where people want to excel and remain. People make companies successful. A clear understanding of what motivates people will help you to achieve extraordinary results. Do not be mistaken in believing that money is the only motivator. It surely helps, but once staff are paid at a reasonable rate, other factors provide the motivation. When employees are happy in their jobs, they remain in their jobs longer and are more committed and loyal to the business. They become important stakeholders and inevitably suggest ways of improving the products and services on offer.

Recognise your employees' efforts and reward them where possible. Let them share in the tangible benefits and experience intangible returns for their efforts. Take opportunities to offer praise and ensure that they know your expectations. Provide feedback and give support, including training, where necessary.

'People' also refers to the other stakeholders in your business. How you interact with your suppliers, partners, competitors and others is also key to your success in getting things done. Sometimes we are keen to tell the plain truth, though it may sound cruel, but sometimes we can achieve a better outcome if we are diplomatic in our delivery of the truth. This is a balancing act and every situation will have to be judged on its own merit.

In considering how to relate to people, it is also important to take into account your suppliers. Duncan Bannatyne, Scottish entrepreneur and investor, makes this crucial point when he indicates that every business must have reliable suppliers who look after you and your customers. You cannot afford to ignore your suppliers who are key stakeholders of your business with some degree of power and influence.

We are in an era of international trade and should consider international norms. As a business professional, you will no doubt encounter individuals from other countries and cultures. Try to familiarise yourself with the business practices of your business associates, suppliers, personnel and other individuals in your supply chain. For example, be prepared to have a meal with

your Latin American counterpart, and ensure you allocate enough time for this activity in your plans. Be prepared to start a meeting as much as an hour late if you are in the Caribbean, but not if you are in Germany.

In effect, 'when in Rome, do as the Romans do' and do not expect them to adjust to your expectations. Respect people for who they are.

Key points:
- ✓ *People are your key assets; treat them with respect.*
- ✓ *Provide your staff with tangible and intangible rewards.*
- ✓ *Familiarise yourself with the business practices of your suppliers, staff and other stakeholders in your business.*

17 Quality

As customers become more sophisticated and better informed, and as their expectations grow, the only way your business can survive and prosper is by offering a commitment to quality. A quality product or service is one that meets customer requirements. Not all customers have the same requirements, so two contrasting products may both be seen as quality products by their users. For example, one house-owner may be happy with a standard light bulb – they would see this as a quality product. Another customer may want an energy-efficient light bulb with a longer life expectancy – this would be their view of quality. Quality can therefore be defined as 'being fit for the customer's purpose'.

When dealing with customers, try to understand what they perceive as quality. How do you do this? Ask them! What do they want? What do they expect? What is their view of your current product or service? Give them samples; spend a little time and effort, gain a lot of feedback in return.

Quality is now expected by consumers and is no longer a point of differentiation. They expect value-added products at competitive prices and competition is fierce in most industries. Remember the golden rule of business – give customers what they want, not what you think they need.

As your business grows, consider acquiring a quality standard. Every organisation should try to improve the way it operates, whether that means increasing profits, driving down costs, increasing market share, managing risk more effectively or improving customer satisfaction.

The implementation of quality standards helps organisations to succeed through improved customer satisfaction, staff motivation and continual improvement.

Quality management systems enhance your image and reputation and are relevant to all organisations whether large or small, public or private, manufacturing or service. They can be applied to a single department right up to a large multinational one. However, if you are prepared to implement them throughout your organisation rather than at particular sites, departments or divisions the benefits will be greater.

There are many recognised standards designed to urge firms to maintain quality and behave ethically. In the same breath, try to have your organisation join your local business network and also the umbrella body of the respective industry in which you are operating. For example, if you are in the business of translation and interpreting, you may want to join the Institute of Translators and Interpreters if you are in the UK. This not only lends credibility to your business, it also raises its profile and reputation and increases your visibility to customers.

In the absence of these standards, the Balanced Scorecard is one of the tools that some businesses use to measure business performance. This tool takes into account the following four key areas and produces a snapshot of how well the business is doing:

1. Learning and growth – takes into consideration the support in place for your team. It focuses on skills development, knowledge creation, training and promotion.

2. Internal business processes – examines the efficiency of the processes that drive your business forward: allocation of resources, your actual products and services.
3. Customer perception – looks at customer satisfaction levels, cost, time management, service and innovation, marketing and promotional activity.
4. Financial growth – reviews measures in place to support profitability, growth, risk assessment and value creation.

Local Chambers of Commerce are good organisations to contact or join, and doing this will enable you to access information to help you keep abreast of good practice within your industry and in business generally.

Key points:
- ✓ *A quality product is one that meets customer requirements.*
- ✓ *Whatever you do, include systems to maintain quality and enhance your organisation's image.*
- ✓ *Consider acquiring a quality standard if this exists in your industry.*

18 Resilience

When Les Brown lost his much-loved radio show, he bounced back; when he had to resign from his job as Ohio State Representative to look after his mother, he bounced back; when he was so broke he had to be living in his office, he bounced back; when he got divorced, he bounced back; though he had to battle prostate cancer, he bounced back and today he is a top motivational speaker who has netted over $1 million per year. Things do get better if you hang in there long enough and put the necessary work into it.

In business you can be knocked down many times. There are many factors lurking that may discourage you and you may even start to doubt whether you made the right decision. It can be a lonely road when you have no idea how the books will balance, whether you will have a large enough cash-flow, whether you will be able to settle your creditors or whether you can survive another month.

Indeed, there may come a time when you cannot see the light and it all seems uphill. There came a time at ACT when we didn't know how we would survive the next few months. Contractors were not subcontracting, our projects had come to an end; the recession was on and there was a lot of uncertainty in the business environment. This was a defining moment and despite the challenges, we persevered. We knocked on new doors, networked more fiercely, undertook more robust marketing and branding and in the process learned a lot and became much more creative and stronger. We did not curl up and die.

Do understand that businesses go through different phases and as long as you are not flogging a dead horse, chances are, they will pass. Analyse the situation and see if you have low market share in a low-growth market. If that is the case you may need to consider diversifying. Use your common sense. Seek guidance from any Supreme Being in which you may believe; if not, rely on your life experience and importantly don't ignore your gut feeling.

Put a strategy into place that will help you to come out of the situation, and stick to it. Get help from those close to you (if they are still there). Speak to your bankers and your creditors and ask them for more time to pay if necessary. Pay your creditors a part of your debt to them – show an intention to settle. Do not hide away and become all stressed about it.

Visionary leaders persist with their ideas, staying with them long enough to make them work. Martin Luther King was stabbed, arrested, jailed and wire-tapped but he had a dream; and nothing could stop him from pursuing that dream. He displayed ultimate resilience, always bouncing back and today he is regarded as one of the most powerful black leaders in American history.

Sir Richard Branson, British business magnate and owner of the Virgin group of companies, started business at sixteen and has had many hurdles along the way but today is worth over £3 billion.

The fact that an initial attempt fails does not mean the idea is a bad one. Those who develop authority on key issues are often those who have had an experience of where it all went wrong. The challenges experienced on the path to growth, the roadblocks, bottlenecks, hills and valleys – when enthusiasm and passion are replaced with despair and uncertainty – are critical hurdles in the quest to achieve a healthy return on investment of time and other resources.

Resilient people keep going because they are grounded in reality and they believe that there is a higher purpose for what they do. They think it is worth getting up after that last fall, brushing themselves off, learning from the experience and getting going again. They have a vision and they focus on that vision. They set milestones and goals and they celebrate small achievements. They possess a clear understanding of their values, strengths and weaknesses, and they seek help from others. When British millionaire entrepreneur Chris Gorman, founder of DX Communications, lost his entire investment of half a million pounds in a recording studio and record label, he bounced back. He went on to earn several million pounds from his internet consultancy and other business ventures. He spoke of his failure as an important learning experience from which he later benefited.

If you have faith in your business, are honest with yourself and have a great attitude, you will survive. The worst thing you can do is panic. That will sap your much-needed energy and you may not have enough to see you through the tough times. Ted Smart, founder of The Book People, explained the meaning of resilience when he said: 'When you start something up, there are times when things go fabulously right and times when they go wrong. You just have to keep your nerve.' He heeded his own advice and today he is a multimillionaire who has earned several awards for his entrepreneurial efforts. The Book People sell over 15 million books a year.

No one said that managing business was all smooth sailing. You must take the good and the bad;

even roses, as sweet as they are, have thorns. When the tough times come, you need to be resilient.

Key points:
- ✓ *Giving up is easy to do.*
- ✓ *There will be challenges, but good leaders stay the course.*
- ✓ *Money is not the key motivator of strong business people, being successful is far more important.*

19   Strategy

Strategy considers the overall objectives of your business and the method you will choose to meet them. If you have a strategy, you have a plan. You must plan in order to minimise your risk of failure; but don't be afraid to alter your plans if circumstances change or if it is clear that you have made an error.

Strategy is developed at varying levels –

- *Corporate strategy* – the overall purpose and scope of the business to meet stakeholder expectations. It is often embodied in the mission statement and decision-making is key at this level.
- *Business unit strategy* – how a business competes in a particular market. It concerns strategic decisions – about product choice, customer service, methodology, gaining market share, maximising opportunities and creating new avenues for development.
- *Operational strategy* – how each part of the business is organised to deliver the corporate business strategies. It focuses on issues such as resources, processes, people and financial allocations.

Irrespective of the level of the strategy, it is important to point out that some intended strategies fail to be

realised while some emergent strategies become realised. Strategies are impacted by the external environment. In developing your strategy think about where are you now, where you want to go and how and when you will get there.

In elaborating a strategy consider:
- Your direction – where is the business trying to get to in the long-term?
- Markets – which markets should a business compete in and what kind of activities are involved in such markets?
- Advantage – how can the business perform better than the competition in those markets?
- Unique Selling Proposition (USP) – what makes you different from existing competitors?
- Resources – what resources (i.e. skills, assets, finance, relationships, technical competence, facilities) do you have, have access to or need to source in order to compete effectively?
- External factors – what environmental factors affect your business' ability to compete (i.e. social, technological, economic, environmental, political, legal, ethical)?
- Stakeholders – who are your stakeholders and what are their values and expectations?

Identifying your key success factors – those factors that must be addressed if you are to succeed – is another important element in formulating your strategy. For example, if you operate a delivery service you may consider flexible delivery times, the speed of the delivery and the price in comparison with your competitors.

Failure is a major propeller for many entrepreneurs. The lessons they learn from failure often allow them to make more prudent decisions in the future.

Sometimes you will need to revisit your strategy as it may need to be updated to include opportunities not observed before or to change one that does not contribute positively to your growth. Flexibility is important in contemporary business management because the factors influencing business are so diverse and unsteady. When Anita Roddick, founder of The Body Shop, found herself with no customers and saddled with a huge empty house with high maintenance costs, she changed her strategy. She turned her house into a residential hotel. The lesson to be learnt is: yes, plan a strategy, but do not be afraid to change course if it is not working.

In formulating your strategy there are management tools which can assist you in analysing your position in the market as well as evaluating the external environment in which you will operate. Following are two such tools with some of the considerations that they evoke:

1. A SWOT Analysis assesses:

Your *Strengths*	What are you good at? How do you know that you are good? Have you ever done it before?
Your *Weaknesses*	What skills do you need (that you don't currently have), do you have

	enough resources, support and contacts?
The *Opportunities*	Have you scanned the business environment to assess existing opportunities? Do you have particular skills and competencies that could enhance your position and market share?
The *Threats*	Is there anything that could hinder your progress or bar your entrance to the market? Who are your competitors?

2. A STEEPLE analysis is used to identify the external forces that impact on a business. It includes the following factors:

Social	Are your products/services suited to the demographics of the location? What is your customer profile?
Technological	What kind of technology exists that could enhance your business; what are your competitors using?
Economic	What is the economic situation in the country? How does this impact on your purchasing power and consumer spending?
Environmental	Are you taking steps to create or sell your product or deliver your service in a more environmentally

	friendly way? How important is 'being green' to your customers?
Political	Is there political support for your product or service? Are there any government policies or initiatives that have an impact on your sector?
Legal	Is there any national or international legislation that is relevant in your industry? Who are the regulatory bodies? Do you understand the law as it relates to employment, competition, consumer protection?
Ethical	Are you aware of the Data Protection Act, do you understand what is expected of your company in respect of fair competition, anti-dumping and general business ethics?

In planning your strategy you must be aware of developments in your respective industry. You cannot afford to make plans without acknowledging changes and trends. Make it your business to keep abreast of developments and plan your strategy accordingly.

Key points:
- ✓ *If you want to reach a destination, you must plan your journey.*
- ✓ *Recognise your SWOT, and USP and study the business environment – competitors, level of demand and STEEPLE factors.*
- ✓ *Change your strategy as necessary and recognise emergent strategies.*
- ✓ *Keep abreast of developments in your industry.*

20 Time Management

All leaders can and should develop great time management skills. A day will always have twenty-four hours and no amount of effort will be able to change that. What we can change however, is how we spend those hours.

The importance of time management is often overlooked in organisations. However, failure to respect time and meet deadlines results in missed opportunities and weakens the bottom line. Time is the master of everything – customers want to be served quickly; you want your workers to complete their tasks in a timely manner; they want to be paid on time, suppliers want to be settled on time, the Inland Revenue gives you a set time to submit your returns, and the list goes on.

Time management is straightforward as long as you commit to it. The key to successful time management is planning and putting systems in place to ensure that the timing is respected. It involves leading by example, identifying and replacing time-wasting systems, and creating a culture within your organisation that respects the value of time. Wasted moments are gone forever along with any return on investment that could have been realised. Take steps to reduce such moments.

There are some time-wasting culprits that you should be aware of: telephone calls, extended tea-breaks, junk mail, unnecessary or poorly planned and chaired meetings, lack of organization, talkative/chatting/ gossiping colleagues, a weak chain of command, interpersonal conflict and a host of other phenomena that are not always immediately obvious.

Often overlooked as major time-wasters is the number of unsolicited mail and telephone calls you receive, especially in the early stages. There are organisations who have learnt the art of accessing company data – they know when you have started your business or when you move to a new area – and they bombard you with their products or services in an attempt to sell to you before others realise the 'opportunity'. You may also receive calls from people who are asking you for donations to various causes and while these may appeal to your generosity, you must remain focused on your business, especially in the early stages. Once you commit to helping these organisations they will always be on your case. If you feel passionately about this, offer a donation and let them go. Otherwise, tell them a polite 'no' and get back to business. Don't be drawn into making pledges at this early stage in your operations.

Manage your time effectively – plan your day, organise yourself or get someone to organise you, be assertive where necessary and learn to say 'no' to tasks. When going through the mail, immediately ditch some things, delegate others and do the rest. Review anything that could be wasting time and effort, particularly habitual tasks, meetings and reports which are produced as a matter of habit. Don't be a slave to a process or system that is simply a waste of time.

Evaluate your activities from time to time to see whether you could do them faster. Automate where possible. Prioritise your tasks in terms of importance and urgency. There are some tasks that may be better left to others, as they may not yield best value for your time.

For example, you may enjoy answering the phone and providing customer service; but consider, is this the best use of your time? Could you be using the time to attract more business to the company?

In your planning, do leave slots for spontaneous activities. You will know when these occur as they have a way of tugging at your gut. These could include a request for a personal meeting from a member of staff or a sudden visit from your spouse. Time is valuable but it should not be saved at the expense of your relationships with others.

Another way to maximise your time is by multi-tasking, e.g. speaking on the phone while making photocopies or stuffing envelopes. Tagging is also a simple and effective way of keeping track of where you are with things. Make a daily to-do list and tick off the ones done by the appointed time.

Dr Wayne Dyer, bestselling author, warned of the ills of not leaving enough time for ourselves when he said: 'Executives in our country are generally loaded with tension and stress. Heart attacks, ulcers and hypertension are considered "normal" in the high-powered institutional levels of business, where employees have little time for their families and "normally" become heavy drinkers, smokers, pill poppers or insomniacs, with no time left over for loving or making love.' The fact is, failure to manage your time causes stress which in turn promotes ill-health and aggravates other conditions.

Time management often requires a commitment to change. The key to successful time management is planning your time and then protecting the planned time. It involves ordering your priorities, reconditioning your environment, and managing the expectations of others.

Businesses suffer, not because they lack resources, but because they mismanage a most important resource – time.

Key points:
- ✓ *Time is a great resource, not to be wasted.*
- ✓ *Planning and organisation are key skills of a good business owner.*
- ✓ *The failure to manage time can cause stress and promote general ill-health.*

21 Uniqueness

Before you start to sell your product or service to anyone else, you should consider, 'would I buy it, and why'? This is especially important if your product or service is very similar to others in your industry. If you are to survive in a competitive market with homogenous competitors, you will need to determine what makes you different, i.e. what is your unique selling proposition (USP)? The culture of an organization is very difficult, if not impossible, to copy. It makes each of our companies unique, but you need to know what it is that you offer that will encourage customers to choose your product or service. If an organisation is to thrive in heated competition it must add value and have something different about it – a unique appeal that sets it apart from other similar offerings.

Identifying your USP requires deep soul searching and creativity. One way to start is by considering what makes you special. You can often find this answer by exploring your motives for setting up the business – what were your thoughts and aspirations? What was the vision that you had? What made you think that you could enter that particular market? What were you hoping to achieve? How do you want to be perceived by customers, competitors and other stakeholders? Will this special aspect of your business motivate customers to buy? Is it believable? Is it truly different from what your competitors are offering? What exactly are you selling? What are the benefits of buying your product? When British entrepreneur Mike Clare spotted a niche in the market for sofa beds he opened the Sofa Bed Centre, selling only sofa beds, which were very popular at the time. He later renamed the company Dreams, which allowed him to diversify his product range. He managed to change focus while maintaining his uniqueness and today his company generates in excess of £100 million in sales per annum.

You may need to put yourself in your customer's shoes. Too often businesspeople are caught up satisfying their own needs and forgetting that it is the customer's needs and wants that they are in business to satisfy. If you don't know what your customers want, don't be afraid to ask them (via surveys and other media available to you). Bear in mind that people buy not only because of price. They consider convenience, quality of customer service and a host of other factors – so don't be forced to drop your price to unsustainable levels in order to compete with more established players.

Once you have considered and answered these questions you will be on your way to establishing your unique selling proposition (USP) – the main benefit or feature of your business, product or service that distinguishes you from other similar businesses. Once you have determined your USP, clear your mind of any preconceived idea about your product or service and be brutally honest for your USP may not necessarily be what you perceive it, or want it to be. Whatever it emerges to be, embrace it and position your business to promote it. If you are still unable to determine what makes your business unique, don't spend time worrying about this. Successful business operation is about making your product stand out, even if the market is crowded with similar items. Set about doing that and your USP will soon emerge. USPs can be determined for individual products or for the business as a whole. They also need to be reviewed regularly (perhaps every two years) to determine whether they are still relevant.

The need to stand out from the crowd is particularly relevant in the current environment of information overflow and hyper-competition. Buyers are overwhelmed by choice, information, ideas, products and services. Choosing among multiple options is usually based on overt or covert differences between offerings. A USP can help customers by saving them time when they are considering buying a product or service. By stating simply and clearly why your product or service is different from others, it will stand out from the competition.

A USP must offer clear benefits or better value. Do not try to fool your customers with short-term benefits because, as renowned singer-songwriter Bob Marley, said, 'You can fool some people sometimes, but you can't fool all the people all the time!' Your USP must be credible and sustainable.

Key points:
- ✓ *There is no point being just another 'kid on the block' you need to stand out from the others!*
- ✓ *Consider what makes you different and promote it.*
- ✓ *Your unique selling proposition must be credible and sustainable.*

22 *Values*

The onus is on the leader to ensure that fundamental values are known and understood throughout the organisation. Everyone must understand their role as well as the *modus operandi* of the organisation. People should know what is expected of them, how they are expected to behave, how they should treat their customers and colleagues and how they should carry out their duties. They should know what the company's mission is – what it is trying to do; the purpose of its existence. Do not assume this is obvious to your staff.

Values are essentially wrapped up in the organisation's culture and refer to the degree of importance you give to something or an ideal accepted by an individual or group. In management parlance the words 'mission' and 'vision' are more commonplace but values also have relevance.

Your mission encapsulates your organisation's purpose – the reason for its existence. The mission statement should be succinct and be familiar to all your stakeholders.

A vision statement defines the aspirations of a company, concentrating on the future and can serve as a source of aspiration for employer and employees alike. Your vision must become a guiding principle for the decisions and actions of your group. If it is not communicated to your team by what you say and do, then you are not true to your vision; indeed you are sabotaging your own organisation. It is *your* driving motivation so drive it and ensure everyone gets a turn at the wheel! What is important is that there is clarity about what the company does, how it does it and why.

Organisations often formulate their value statements around a number of factors including:

- The importance they place on integrity and ethics.
- How they treat their employees – opportunities for promotion, personal development and training.
- How they treat their customers – how they manage customer satisfaction, how they provide their services, the after-care they provide and the entire customer experience.
- Their relationship with shareholders and stakeholders.
- Their willingness to learn.
- How they use technology to propel growth.
- Their role in the social and economic development of the communities in which they operate.
- Their approach to creativity and innovation.
- Their attitude to success.

Communicating your values is not simply a case of hanging it in a frame on your office wall but rather bringing the whole team to perceive your vision and begin to share it with you. Lead by example and your staff will follow. Bear in mind that your team will be expected to adhere to the values and thus the culture that you are trying to cultivate, even if that culture conflicts with their personal values. You must be prepared to manage these eventualities early and avoid the need to resort to curative measures such as the use of sanctions.

Business is not about winning at all costs. Deals where both parties feel that they have 'won' are more sustainable than those where either party feels cheated. Employees who are well informed will be in a better position to offer good customer service and satisfy the business objectives of the company, thus assisting it to achieve its goals. If they share your vision they are more likely to help you achieve it.

Key points:
✓ *As an organisation you must know clearly what you stand for – what is acceptable and what is not.*
✓ *To be effective, values must be communicated to all concerned.*
✓ *A win-win solution is far more sustainable than a win-lose outcome.*

23 *Wisdom*

Wisdom must be distinguished from knowledge. Knowledge is the ability to arrange, assess, define, duplicate, label, list, memorise, name, order, recall, recognise, relate, repeat and reproduce information. Wisdom reaches beyond the information to see inner qualities and relationships not immediately apparent.

Being wise will also assist you to maintain your competitive advantage. Keep abreast of what is happening in your industry; keep an eye on your competitors, learn from them and don't allow complacency to set in. We can only be overtaken if we are ahead. Use market intelligence continually; collect data from customers, your staff and even family members.

In your business you will encounter situations that are not leaning either right or left; situations where creative thought and common sense must prevail in order to see the trees through the woods. You may plan a course of action, dotting all the Is and crossing all the Ts but at the last minute you find that you have to change dramatically.

For example, two of us from ACT attended a meeting in order to negotiate a contract. We knew what we were going to propose and what we expected to hear. During the meeting we found that the other party was on a totally different tangent, looking for something dissimilar. But it was a tangent on which, with some innovation, we could deliver. What do you think we did? In this situation a mental assessment of the situation needs to be done quickly – ask yourself: Will we still benefit from this new arrangement? Can we deliver the product and if not, do I know someone who can? Could this be a window of opportunity for me to expand into this field or is it a downright impossibility at this time? All of that has to be decided in a split second so you have to know your industry, the possibilities, your ability and the rest is down to gut feeling. The way you respond to your contractors at that moment can decide whether you seize a new opportunity or leave it for someone else. At the same time you have to be careful with your tone and body language, taking into consideration that you are not alone at the meeting and you are taking decisions on behalf of your colleagues. ACT got the contract and it enabled us to develop a new product and tap into a totally new, growing market.

Wisdom is different from honesty. In the above scenario you can either choose to be honest and say, 'we have never done this before,' and risk losing an opportunity which you may well have been able to satisfy, or you can say, 'our workforce has a wide range of skills and I am certain that we will be able to deliver,' and win the business. The first answer is honest, the second is wise. You have the choice.

One of the key responsibilities for entrepreneurs is to make decisions. The making of sound decisions will impact positively on performance and ultimately on profitability. Using wisdom in your decision-making processes shows good leadership and raises your profile. More importantly, it earns you respect and enables you to maximise your opportunities.

Theo Paphitis, Cypriot retail expert, presents the concept of the busy fool – someone who takes on a project and pumps in resources although they know in their gut that it is never going to be a financial success. That could be a case of the heart ruling the head; not a good example of wisdom.

'Wisdom begets knowledge, knowledge begets wisdom'[1]. Learn as much as you can from anywhere that you can. Be realistic in your expectations and never promise what you cannot deliver. Tap into the tacit knowledge of your staff, and give praise where it is due. Do not overestimate your capabilities but do not underestimate them either. Use your intuition and gut feeling but never with reckless abandon. It is dangerous to ignore your intuition because if it doesn't feel right, it usually isn't.

Be smart enough to know when it's time to go and don't allow yourself to be thrown out of the market or dropped by a contractor because of non-compliance or incompetence, perceived or real. If you have made a decision that clearly turns out to be wrong, and you recognise this, don't hesitate to change course, despite your ego. To avoid bad decisions, take time to plan and collect key information, and put pen to paper. Avoid making decisions based solely on emotions, and in business, try to be objective.

---

[1] 1 John William McGrath III (http://www.dreamagic.com/cgi-bin/PoetryGen.cgi?author=John_William_McGrath_III&html=mcgrath1_25&title=Profundity&number=2553)

Key points:
- ✓ *Wisdom begets knowledge and knowledge begets wisdom.*
- ✓ *Wisdom helps you to think on your feet when you find yourself having to make unprogrammed decisions.*
- ✓ *Wisdom earns you respect and enables you to maximise opportunities.*

24 X-ray Vision

X-rays are usually used to detect conditions not visible to the naked eye. In business you need to develop x-ray vision. Do see the obvious things, but see the invisible ones, too. The big things that you see – the profits, the customer satisfaction, the growth in the organisation – are made of the little, often invisible ones – effort, dedication, loyalty, thought processes, innate ability, skill. Learn to recognise the things that are not said and devise ways of keeping your staff motivated.

Too often, senior managers go hunting for talent when it is right under their noses. This practice can be dangerous and damaging to the organisation. It decreases motivational levels, encourages under-currents, leads to high staff turnover and a broken synergy.

You will not be able to see everything, but you can see through the eyes of others. Do not encourage gossip; rather, promote open discussion between warring factions if they emerge. Close down arguments early and get back to business but ensure that those concerned have had an opportunity to have their say and all parties understand and agree to the solution generated.

Get into the habit of developing your people. Pursue quality standards and seek out development opportunities for your staff and yourself. Visit your staff and speak to them. Ascertain their feelings and express appreciation for what they are doing. You will learn more about them if they see and regard you as 'human'. You will pick up ideas on how to effect improvements. Take these on board and give praise where it is due. Your staff will be far more willing to go the extra mile to make things work if they feel that it was their idea. There is no need to compete with the staff for ideas. Take a good idea and make it work, regardless of its source. In summary, recognise the hidden talents within your organisation and reward them. If you don't, someone else will.

Standing back at times and taking a *helicopter view* of the organisation is absolutely necessary. It enables entrepreneurs to assess their businesses and, if they are truly honest with themselves, they may see where improvements need to be made and take steps to make them. It allows them to determine whether their plans are working and if they need to be changed. The trouble is, too often businesspeople take only that view and fail to view the situation from the ground where ordinary people operate. It is all well and good to see through the eyes of your senior staff but be mindful of personal agendas, prejudices, biases and other background information to which you may not be privy.

As your organisation grows you will need to delegate responsibilities but be careful not to do this too early and lose sight of the core of your business. Be aware of your key functions and processes. If you are not an expert in your field of business, try to acquire an understanding of how things work. For example, if you are in the education business, develop a working knowledge of the workflow. What happens from the time that a client is enrolled to the time he completes his course and beyond. Be particularly keen to understand the processes that relate to staff recruitment, performance management systems, rewards and incentives, employment regula-tions, training and development, promotion, change management, and so on. As you grow, be careful not to outgrow the organisation so that it becomes foreign to you. Treat it as your baby; always know what's happening with her.

The ability to look deeper into ideas also brings benefits as the true entrepreneur sees opportunities where others don't. Look beyond the basic idea and consider: 'what if X were the case? What else could it mean?' Stretch your imagination and use metaphors to develop new ideas.

In summary, pay attention to detail, protect your human assets and use your imagination.

Key points:
- ✓ *The big things – profit, customer satisfaction, growth... are made of the smaller things – effort, dedication, loyalty, ability, skill ...*
- ✓ *Recognise the things that are not said and keep your staff motivated.*
- ✓ *Recognise and appreciate your human assets – they are key to your business success.*

25 *Youth*

The concept of youth here is two-fold. Firstly, it embraces the willingness to try new ways of working. Too often business people get stuck in a routine, using tried and tested means to achieve their goals. They fail to encourage creativity or to embrace new technologies and new ideas. They develop a 'not invented here' syndrome which basically stifles creativity and, by extension, curbs innovation and growth.

If you were fortunate enough to inherit a business, you are at risk of this phenomenon developing. This is because the business would have been operating according to a particular culture over time and it may be time to change in light of the evolving external environment. We have already established that culture is particularly difficult to change.

When you inherit employees who have worked with your father and perhaps your grandfather over many years, and who are deeply rooted in their ways, it is extremely difficult to introduce new ideas or ways of working without causing pain on both sides.

In some cases you may find that you have to make employees redundant and they may equate losing their job with losing their right leg. You must remember that in many cases the job defined them, dictated how they spent their lives, when they had their children and holds other memories. Indeed it could be like losing a beloved family member. There is no magic in bearing bad news and only you will be able to determine how you do this if it becomes necessary. This is a situation where the heart may try to overrule the head. Just keep your focus and determine what is important to you at this time of your life. Try not to make enemies but you must be prudent.

Offer a cushion e.g. redundancy pay, some perks, introduction to another job opportunity, a work reference or something that will soften the blow to employees if they have to go. Laying off people should be a last resort and should only be done where efforts to retrain or redeploy fail. You should also make every effort to adapt the work environment to encourage your loyal workers to stay.

The second concept of youth is the need to engage young people in your company. If you are unable to employ them, then at least offer work experience opportunities to college students, and give them responsibility. With proper guidance and training they can develop true competence and you will benefit from their creativity and freshness. Once they are able, empower them with tasks and grant them some degree of autonomy. It is amazing what young people can do if they feel motivated and encouraged to do it.

By employing young people your organisation will benefit in two ways: it will have ideas that might otherwise go unnoticed which could bring true innovation to the company. Secondly, you will be providing opportunities for learning and employment within the community and thus satisfying your social responsibility. Another benefit that is often overlooked is the fact that learning takes place on both sides: the young person learns and the entrepreneur also learns; indeed the organisation also learns. Too often companies fail to see this as a learning opportunity and fail to grasp it. Although some work placement opportunities go wrong, the majority of them bring mutual benefits to the organisation and the learner.

Welcome age and experience but make place for youth and innovation, thus enriching your organizational culture and boosting staff learning and retention. Do not let the fear of poaching by your competitors prevent you from engaging youth for if you build a unique, morale-boosting culture in your company it will be impossible to copy and your employees and trainees will experience job satisfaction and will be more likely to remain with you, even in difficult times.

Key points:
- ✓ *Try new ways of working and avoid getting stuck in routines.*
- ✓ *Welcome age and experience but make place for youth and innovation.*
- ✓ *Offer opportunities for training and work experience – this will have a two-fold advantage – to the company and to the individual.*

26 Zest

If you have decided to embark on a business path, you will need plenty of energy as you will find yourself doing a lot of the groundwork. Try to maintain a healthy lifestyle through diet and exercise. Not only will you need to work long hours, you will also have to be enthusiastic about the work, driven by your desire to excel. Do not take for granted that you can simply hire a manager and all will be taken care of, despite how much money you may have or how much you may be paying this person.

If you are in business in an area in which you are trained, let the business benefit from your expertise. If you know nothing about the business, then it's time to learn something about it. What you cannot do is simply expect it to grow on its own without putting in at least the initial groundwork for this to happen. Even after your business has taken off, do spend time with your staff at varying levels to understand the operational level and job satisfaction. In this way you are able to identify problems that may exist or may be waiting to happen and you can deal with these early. Do not expect your top managers to deal with everything effectively or for them to tell you everything. On the other hand, do not expect to be able to deal with everything yourself; you also need to listen – and listen to everyone – not just your managers.

Identify ways of living the customer experience. Call your company and see how quickly calls are answered, for example.

There is always something to do when you are running a business, irrespective of the level of staffing you may have. Put some energy into the groundwork and maintain that energy, and the chances are you will get even more back than you have put in.

It is also important you radiate positive energy into your business. You will come upon hard times but you will need to keep the faith and continue ploughing on. You will also meet friends and family members who laugh at you for trying; they will encourage you to go and find a 'good job', avoid the 'headaches'. If you are convinced you are following your heart's desire, keep going regardless.

You must be positive about what you are doing. In exuding positive energy you must exercise empathy and be non-judgemental toward others. You will learn from your mistakes so do not be too hard on yourself for making them in the first place. You will develop confidence and inner peace that will help you take criticisms and give you the strength to weather the storms. There is no place for an ogre-type dictator in contemporary workplaces. Replace that with a consultative kind of leadership, valuing the human assets for which you pay so dearly. Learn how to be assertive when necessary, but never aggressive.

If you enjoy your business it will be easier to spend long hours at it. Some entrepreneurs are scared of failure and that makes them find the energy to keep going. Sarah Doukas, founder of Storm modelling agency is one of these. She has a fear of failure but she also loves what she does. It is that love and motivation that enabled her to be the success that she is today.

Exerting energy is about playing your part in the process; sowing good seed and reaping the harvest alongside your workers. It is about leading from in front, setting an example for others and being true to your ambition. It is about being flexible and responsive to the needs of your staff, customers and other key stakeholders. It is about being able to adapt to changing circumstances and motivating your team to share your vision. It is about having the passion, inner strength and self-discipline that will allow you to take care of your body and to refrain from self-destructive behaviours that can impair your performance. It is about preserving your enthusiasm even when you have to go the extra mile.

Key points:
- ✓ **Satisfaction comes from you playing your part in the business, leading from in front, motivating your workers and reaping the harvest alongside them.**
- ✓ **You will need to take care of your body if you are to go the extra mile.**
- ✓ **Remain heavily involved in your business; do not expect that your staff will take over and make it happen without you!**

Bibliography

BBC (various authors), *Dragons' Den, Success from Pitch to Profit* (HarperCollins, 2008), pp. 3–70.

Bridge, Rachel - *How I Made It* (Kogan Page, 2007), pp. 70, 73, 96, 106.

Brown, Les - *Live your Dreams* (HarperCollins Audio, 1994), p. 35.

Brown, Les - *It's Not Over Until You Win* (Simon & Schuster, 1998), p. 104.

Carnegie, Dale - *How to Win Friends and Influence People* (Vermilion, 2002), p. 53.

Dyer, Dr Wayne - *Pulling Your Own Strings* (HarperCollins, 2001), pp. 171.

Gabler, Neal - *Biography of Walt Disney* (Vintage, 2007).

Harmer, Harry - *Martin Luther King* (The History Press, 1998), pp. vii–xiii.

Robbins, Anthony - *Notes from a Friend* (Simon & Schuster, 995), p. 23.

Roddick, Anita - *Business as Unusual* (Thorsons, 2005), pp. 34–35.

Semler, Ricardo - *Maverick* (Arrow Books, 1994), pp. 5, 106.

Semler, Ricardo, *The Seven Day Weekend* (Arrow Books, 2003), pp. 66, 205.

People Index